Being
in Two Volumes

Also by Ruby Harmon

Poetic Moves While Doctoring

BEING
IN TWO VOLUMES

POEMS BY
RUBY M. HARMON

POETIC MOVES PUBLISHING
New York

© Copyright 2009 by Ruby M. Harmon.

All rights reserved. Printed in the United States of America. No part of this book may be transmitted or reproduced by any means, electronic or mechanical, without written permission of the author or publisher, except for quotations included in reviews.

ISBN 10   0-9824277-0-0
ISBN 13   978-0-0824277-0-5

Published by Poetic Moves Publishing
P.O. Box 630106
Bronx, NY 10463

Table of Contents

Balancing Act

Simply Ears	12
At Avenue C	13
Light Upside Down	14
He and She (IV)	15
Water	16
Labor of Love	17
Birth Order	18
Goal Driven	19
Seeing Snowflakes	20
Rush Hour Commute	21
Balancing Act	22
Randomly Chosen	23
Shhh…	24
Please	25
And So the Sun	26
Handiwork	27
He and She (V)	28
The Why of Who	29
Untitled I.	30
Untitled II.	31
Tourist to Native	32
The Dance as we Know It	33
Delaying Catastrophe	34
Father and Daughter	36
She Defined?	37
Chalk and Cheese	38
Allowing Her	39
Sunday School Again	40
Art	41
To Read the Words	42
Ma Coccinelle	44
Patient and Doctor	45
Wishing Well	46
Comfort Junk	47
A Fly Like Us	48
Thus Sprach Die Musik	49
Again and Again	50

Her Choice	51
Standing Misunderstood	52
Sparse	53
Time Waits	54
To the Youngest Member, Number 27254-1	56
Rootless	57
He and She (VI)	58
To Her Life	59
Stealing Life for Life	60
Dentally Speaking	61
It's All Relative To Whom/Realization I	62
Connected	64
Untitled VIII/Connected Two	65
Comfort	66
Comfort Two	67
Leaning Tree	68
The Exodus of Here	69
Choices	70
Awaiting Entry	71
...And So the Promise Was	72
Renewal	73
The Dream	74
Too Long It's Been	75
Tête-A-Tête	76
Speaking of Leopards	77
We Know Her Everywhere	78
Foottalk	79
A Near Collision With Nuns	80
What the Birds Tell the Bees	81
White Roses	82
Hiatus Foregone	83
Reminders	84
For Whom	85
Ned	86
Don't Speak Twice	88
Aging	90
Grazing Out of the Fold	91
Spellbound	92
Reminders II	93
Work in Progress	94

Exchanging Pleasantries

Challenged on Hillsborough/Artful Endurance	98
Made-Up	100
Cemented Inertia	101
Not Always Easy to Ignore	102
Cool Draft	103
Couched Therapy	104
Pressing Onwards	105
Golden Lotuses	106
The Miracle of You	108
Moon Peace	109
Adolescence Calls	110
Since Seven	112
Untitled V	113
Adjusting the Focus	114
Exchanging Pleasantries	115
Foliage Unveiled	116
Thoughts on Religion	117
Create	118
What Was, Is	119
Oxygen Rocks	120
Gossip Collage	121
Like Love	122
Frustration	123
It Ain't Illegal	124
Worldly Thoughts	125
Perceptions	126
The Small Divide	127
Kiss Goodnight	128
Dust to Dust	129
Neutral Delight	130
The Call Girl as Parasomniac	131
Colère	132
Retreat	133
Tainted	134
Birds Like Us	136
Honey to Me	137
The Bath Call I	138
Welcome Life I	139
Seeing the Gold Coast	140
Refugee Camp	142
The Mule	144
Oasis	146
Presently Present	147

Welcome Life II	148
The Bath Call II	149
Soulful Playing	150
Untitled VI	151
The Eye's Mind	152
27 Years	153
Inadvertent Mixing	154
A Pearl in Waiting	155
A Kiss is Not A Kiss	156
Beauty in Wood	157
On Seeing the Doctor	158
What an Orange Reveals	160
Doctor and Patient	161
Thinking in Vain	162
40 and ...	163
Chances Are...	164
Fear Moves Slowly	165
Doctor and Patient 2	166
Champagne Slingbacks	167
Love-Joy	168
Patient and Doctor	169
Doctor and Patient 3	170
Whose Realm?	171
Red River Running	172
Treasured Truth	173
The Invitation	174
The Question	175
Life As Dance	176
Bone Cry	177
Hearing Her	178
Morning Routine	179
Engaged	180
Nothing Quite Like It	181
Wishing You Here	182
Questioning You, Questioning Me	183
Fifth Grade Blues	184
Wishing You Here (#2)	185
Heat Rising	186
Class Reunion	188
Late Night Driving	190
Son to Father	191
Defiance	192
Literary Groove	193
Well?	194

DEDICATION

As always, to my wonderful mother, Queen Mary:
You are an inspiration! I love you.

To marietjewelgmakahnvaniamonaauntireneverity:
With appreciation, love and thanks!

To Daddy: We love and miss you.

To LOVE.

Balancing Act

SIMPLY EARS

His ears stand
Enormous receptacles accepting sound
Embracing the entirety of his head
Nearly one-fifth the width across his countenance
Curved into narrow canals
Protector of a world concealed
Of drums
Of balance
Of hair cells
And vibrations
Of oceans
Of complex spiral chambers
Interpreting waves
Of delicate ossicles
And neuronal circuits
Orchestrating and translating sounds

And he seems oblivious
Standing there
Pretending not to hear me
Despite the enormity of those auricles
That announce his presence
Several decibels
Away...

AT AVENUE C

His off-duty light was lit
And still he was flagged
By a seemingly well-to-do couple
"75th and Park to Alphabet City"

Watching them chat, he obviously attentive to her
Reflected from the rearview mirror
Smiling, laughing, winding their way through traffic
A quick twenty five dollars...

And now arriving there
At Avenue C
Their dumbfounded looks playing Ping-Pong
Him to her to him
And he lying about forgetting or losing his wallet
Whispering to her...

Both he and she abruptly exiting the cab
Running down the street
The cabbie screaming, ranting
Epithets flying
In hot pursuit
And they, now, slowing their pace
Calling him a foreigner, a stalker
A liar—imagine that!

How audacious, these two
As they opened their apartment's entrance
Closing the door in his face; then bursting
      into laughter
Their laughter augmenting his anger
Heat rising from his pores

How ironic, he thought, being taken for a ride
Duped from 75th and Park to Avenue C

LIGHT UPSIDE DOWN

Upside down, the glimmer of light
Meets my eyes
In cool melon and pink grapefruit hues
Reflected on the corner wooden table
In linear bisecting dots

The blinds drawn
The organza window dressing
Allowing me these geometric
Pastel reflections
On the corner wooden table

The simple beauty that is
Nurtures my eyes
Upside down
Laying supine

Lost in the moment, my ears
Deafened to the sirens, horns and
        passersby outside,
I can create
Daydream a poem, song
Privy to the wonderful properties
Of sun
Light

HE AND SHE (IV)

He says
His joints are as worn
As the rusty hinges of that ninety-year-old barn.
She says
His aches speak of generations
Of lifting, picking, hauling, shucking
Carrying weight
His palms callused
His fingers curved
The right fifth severed since childhood.

He tells of working the railroads;
She hums old spirituals
That carried them through.
Hardships seemed a dime a dozen then
But faith fought their battles.

She quilts still at 84.
Flying geese meant more back then
Secrets locked in fabric and thread
Elusive to those who thought
Them simplistic.

His wrinkles are as hers:
Carved deeply
In rich mahogany skin.
He still works at 90
Picking and hauling
174 years of humbled history.

He and she
Still legends in the making.

WATER

They say I am
Ninety-eight percent water
Fluid movements stored
In mass
And so
I imagine me
In oceans
Water slicing water
Ubiquitous in me
And nature

I imagine me
Relishing in this reality
Of me
In me
Around me

I imagine me
As water
Clearly,
I am nature

LABOR OF LOVE

The roundness that is her
Pushes out
With little feet kicking
Curled inside, against the liquid warmth.

And each beat,
Beats in time
Soon to face the earth
In days

This living she feels
Against her hand
Moves restless with each breath;
Awaiting the inevitable
Push
With every ounce of strength
Crowning two the new joys
That came through labor.

Breathing outside the womb
Against her face,
Their vernix shows
That beauty comes from within;
Their cries proclaim
This a labor of love.

BIRTH ORDER

Her purpose here
May not be to birth life,
Rather to enable living
For the souls who choose
To come this way.

Though the chatter rings loudly
And the gazes question,
Curiosity whispers
As time passes
And she ponders
The fruitfulness of her womb

Ultimately,
She learns that

The completeness of a woman
Is indeed more complex
Than birthing a child

And so, she smiles...

GOAL DRIVEN

He lunges left   right
Left
In black and white
The netting echoing his moves
The momentum palpable
In the ahs

The moment seems surreal
With black and white and red
Deliberately running en masse

His body swerves
The choreography elegant
Beads of sweat somersault randomly down his face

Solo, with mind steadfast
Eyeing the patched black and white swiftness
Accelerating towards him
Voices stay silent
Awaiting their ultimate defender
Whose goal remains only to prevent a goal

His leathered palm reaches high
Encompassing the ball

In the sweltering heat, the world watches him
In awe

SEEING SNOWFLAKES

What marvel leaves you entranced?
Clear, cool icicles touching skin
Never thought complex
Quickly melting away

Uniqueness created in moisture
Nature's geometry represented as hexagons
Visible as snowflakes

Open your mouths to taste it
Instantly cool, then evaporating
Roll in its accumulation
Packed firm

Appreciate the amazing properties of water
As snow
Flakes in glorious symmetry
F   a
           l   l
   i   n
               g

What a marvelous gift of nature

Behold!

RUSH HOUR COMMUTE

They stood and sat
Shoulder to shoulder
          kcaB-Back
                  Knee to knee
Mouths dancing in Urdu, Spanish, English
Against the background screech
Of metal to metal
And words tumbling from speakers overhead

These trains were newer, sleeker
Purportedly more comfortable
Despite smaller seats
The metal walls spared the creative signatures
Of urban youth

In the crowd
Two argued vehemently
As one wiggled uncomfortably into a nearby seat
Another bobbed his head intently to music
Only present in his mind

The intimacy of strangers here,
Forced in this rush hour commute
Where most avoided eye contact,
Was simply ironic

Thankfully, this time
The air conditioner worked
For if they had to be this close
At least, they were playing it cool

BALANCING ACT

I purposefully chose the broadest waxed leaf
Placing the tiny cookie crumb there
Knowing quite well that the ant would visit

Wanting to witness the tiny creature
In an act of balance,
I waited patiently
To see her
Inch underneath the parcel of food
Balancing, as though weightless
The crumbly speck on her back,
There for all to see,
Running the risk of being robbed

Her tiny steps cautious
Down the stem
Where others waited
To indulge in the treasured feast
Propped carefully on her back.

I watched her disappear
Under the shelter of even broader leaves
Amazed at how effortless the task seemed

In this moment, she seemed herculean
Gracefully, carrying the load

RANDOMLY CHOSEN

"Your phone number was chosen
Randomly

For a burial plot at..."
The ease with which she spoke the words
Cast doubt on its validity
But the caller id listed Greenbriar Cemetery
"Not interested"
My usual response to telemarketers;
Half-thinking this a practical joke
Or just plain old public relations

       Forced to confront mortality
       The physical end of being here
       as we know it
       Being laid to rest

She offered the reservation too prematurely
Her tone banal

          Pensive on the why and how of being called
          Pondering the randomness of the call

The proposition intended   to drum up business

Telemarketing was presenting burials
      Like magazine subscriptions

I thought

Shhh…

Sleep comes
    Abruptly
        Through heavy eyes
            With confusion evolving
            into peace

Resting
    The weighted life succumbs stubbornly
        Dancing asleep in its cornucopia
        Of dreams

PLEASE

He chose to plead with her
Affectionately
As if pleasing her
Seemed the one
Valiant thing to do

The time had come and gone
Quickly
Diminishing what had felt
Magnanimous then

Please
Listen
Wait...

The words echoing a realness so tangible
To solder the fragile links
That kept them
One
Privately

And what had felt indefensible then

Evaporated
Pleasingly to both

AND SO THE SUN

Have you thought the sun
A star
With eyes fixed
Deciphering the energy that heals
And scorches

Can you fathom the sun
A god
Universal energy
RA-DIANT
Fostering life

In times of Heliopolis and now?

And what of the sun and moon
In courtship
Suitors eclipsing each other's brilliance
A marvel to behold!
Cautiously

The sun alone
At night, surrenders to darkness
Folding beyond the horizon
In hours, rising awake at dawn

HANDIWORK

These hands work magic
Mapping out isles of rough terrain
As cartographers would
Tracing paths undiscovered
On this archipelago
Of extinct wild and tamed nature
Colorful, vibrant, exotic

This ancient art form
    Of charting valleys, oases
    Oceans – azure and serene
    Of barren deserts
    And chiseled canyons against burnt
        auburn sunsets
    Of lush, vibrant foliage
    And miles and miles of nearly transparent frost

Of hands deftly skilled,
    Dancing with fingertips

Stepping lightly then deep,
Allows a deep complacency
That the recipient profoundly feels
And surely the giver senses

HE AND SHE (V)

It felt like cotton
On his nape
Each strand bolted upright
A whispered chill lingered
Under the warmth of her palm

The soft, gentle perfumed
Hand laid there
Its tapered elegance placed
Gracefully over the bony prominence
That begged for warmth

His hand explored hers gently
Bringing it to receive words
Against his lips
And she enclosed each word
Purposefully
Carrying it within

And soon each other their hands would find
Drawn together
Held tapered and callused
Palm to palm
He and she
Letting the moment endure
Seconds, minutes, hours...

THE WHY OF WHO

People stare
At her
Nameless, homeless, purposeful
Hopeful in her world
Though pitied in their short-sightedness
Of seeing only skin deep
And never exchanging words,
Vowels, utterances with,
though willingly doing so about,
her
As though invisible
She were

And one or two
May offer food
Change, dollars
Half-questioning her choice to spend it
For sustenance or hallucinogens

But
Dare they speak with her
And hear her recite
Her story of immigration, education, wealth,
 eviction, depression and motivation,
They would see
A face determined to defy prejudices
And create a new beginning

UNTITLED

I.

Isis speaks
From a fertile tongue
Watered so effortlessly
Drinking of the Nile
Her bosoms as pyramids
Her eyes radiant as rubies

The eunuch stands afar
The choice of progeny

No longer his
Usurped under the shadow
Of duty

And she smiles at him
Not desiring more than simple courtesy

His eyes stare
Antagonistically
Attempting to decipher
The mystery that she speaks

Carving her body
Language into hieroglyphs
He secures the images deep
In his eye's mind

II.

Oh, how they drink
From grapes
The sweet sap
They who honor you, Dionysus
Sprung from the limb of Zeus

Women danced ecstatically
Celebrating you—
Who could imbue and inspire creativity
Through drink and song
Ripening the mind
Liberating through chaos

Is it mythical, your history?

Dionysus,
Greek deity of fertility and enology
What do you epitomize—?
That some should recite dithyrambs, blissfully
And others proclaim you rebel?
What do you symbolize—?
That your legend has survived mysteriously
Despite the controversy

TOURIST TO NATIVE

She is of this region
Where the sun beats on the back
Deepening the darkness
Of melanin-toned skin
And salty water streams
Necessarily moistening the heated humanness

And so she watches
Others basking in the glorious sunlight
Nearly nude
Exposed and sprawled on ocean blue
Recliners
Eyes concealed behind sepia shades

And they survey her
Rich chocolate brown-ness
Covered in loose garments
Walking away from the very sun
That some covet
Her bare feet indenting the sand
The straw fedora barely shielding her eyes

This brilliance
This energy is what attracts most to this land
Of seashell-colored sand
And azure waters
Basking in the glorious sunlight
This land draws them like a magnet
Its beauty abundant
Indeed plenteous to share

THE DANCE AS WE KNOW IT

And one foot propped
Atop the other
She wiggles and twists
Her body expressing the rhythm
From foot to foot
The dance recognizable
Incited by the fullness
And urgency that she feels now

Barely standing
Fourth in line
She waits anxiously
Dancing

And though they acknowledge
The need to let the water run

Unimpeded
No one offers her place

DELAYING CATASTROPHE

His hand shook vigorously
As did my heart
Tremble in its protective covering
His hand unstable
Holding the revolver just inches
From my head

His fear evidently external
Mine internal
Both somatic
The two nearly colliding
Igniting catastrophe
Yet, despite this, calmness floated
From my lips
And compassion from my heart

Our eyes met briefly
I, hoping he could not read
The fright in mine

It seemed time stood still until
He waved me on,

Then fired

My back turned
Not sure who had been struck
He, the air or I
But within seconds, my hand found
    the one lifeline

My fingers dialed nine-one-one

Then again,
Shots rang loudly
The air, the police, he or I

My pace became brisker, obviously unharmed
Hearing voices trailing behind me
And muted footsteps
I turned
Hesitantly

Witnessing the police beckon
Refusing to shoot
Him taunting them

Another two gunshots rang loudly
From his revolvered hand
Catapulted into his trembling heart

And soon
It ended
His fears colliding
Igniting catastrophically
Suffocated in this abyss

Time moved quickly

I looked up
And graciously whispered a prayer skyward

My life had been spared!

FATHER AND DAUGHTER

His body has gone ballistic again
And there is no intelligible speech
Though he laughed right before

...How ironic the prelude...

His body shakes uncontrollably
And reflexively, she reaches her little hand
To gently touch his cheek
Magical thinking in her four-year-old world
Of effecting change by touch
Not impossible this thought:
The chance to change involuntary movement
Through voluntary touch

But this time, the jerking lasts
Longer and longer
She shakes him
To awaken
And kisses his hand
Now quieted
And cries
And stares
Repeating the actions in no particular order

And as he opens his eyes
Fatigued, dazed
Reality re-emerges

She touches his cheek
And kisses his hand
"Daddy, daddy...awake,"
She smiles and hugs him tightly

SHE DEFINED?

There is a sexiness to her
Soulfulness
In speak and dress
Not trying
Just actively being
In her connected-ness to spirit
To oneness

True, simple, intentional living
Emanates, vibrates from the core within
Not obstreperous
Nor egotistical
Empathic to living things
Without judgement

She remains an enigma
To many
Grounded, she is

CHALK AND CHEESE

"Like chalk and cheese..."

Who questioned their distance then?
Amidst the I do's, gold rings, hoorahs
And champagne and lace
The conformity that epitomized their love
Glued them as one then

The space between so schismatic
Now
And yet they like each other better
Now
With the love having spilled out
Over time
And the differences accepted

The glaring fact is
The two are now more similar
In deeds and words
Despite their obvious differences

And indeed some cheeses taste
Like chalk
And some chalks resemble cheese
So there...

Like chalk and cheese
These two remain separate in sameness

ALLOWING HER –*for Susan*

She would like to speak
Of the joys in days and hurt
Of the life in now
And being that she struggles to comprehend
But she signals her voice
Too parched
Though some hear her loudly
Fighting and acquiescing all at once

And for those of her
And those who came through
Her
She stares, as though betrayed
Her courage dampened
And faith diluted
By pain and blame
That need not be present

So for today
Shower her with love
Standing positively united
As a pillar

Uplifting her tiredness
Bolstering her strength

Compassion need be present
Allowing her to speak
Of hurt and joys and love and fear
And yes, peace

One by one or
All at once

SUNDAY SCHOOL AGAIN

Mama's fingers deftly weave
Plaits in threes
And bows and baubles frame her
Work routinely

The dress, baby blue, pleated
Stops shy of the knees
The bodice fitting what
Would be hips

Today calls for patent leather
To complete the look

At 9, the little one has a sense of style
On Sundays
At 10, the organ pipes out
"What a friend we have in Jesus, all our..."
The hallelujahs exalt
The heads sway
Voices waft high
In this little brick edifice
Almost bursting at the seams

"Rejoice and be glad..."
The purple-robed conductor proclaims

And she and nine others sit
Eager to learn what the word
Save-your truly means.

ART *–for Uncle Fritz*

His art

      moves me
      strikes me
      delights me
      and awakens with indigo
      yellow red splashes of life
      stroked on canvas

        His art

      comforts me
      uplifts with hope
      tie-dyed in fabric
      with earth-toned hues

            what joy the creativity
            must bring to him
            what creative potential
            his art unearths for me

                without knowing...

TO READ THE WORDS

Dear Margaret,
It's been years since we spoke.
You never write and since I don't have a phone,
        I never call.
This may be my last letter to you
        but I trust that you are well.
Love,
Mitchell

She has pretended this long
To read the words and know the letters
And though she speaks well
Enough
To read
The words have never stuck
In the recesses of her mind

In times past, leaving elementary school to work
To feed the hungry lips
That later thanked her endlessly was commonplace,
Even expected
And Mitchell would tease her because he liked her,
even at such a young age
For that is what young boys do

Oh Mitchell,
If only you knew that I don't know to put pen
        to paper, or recite the words written there...
Your letters are all stacked neatly in my
        favorite shoebox with ribbon trimmings,
        for I treasure them all...

Back then, school was to pass the time
While we waited to work

My good friend, Mildred, insists it's never too late
So I've learned twenty letters and ninety words
       including dyslexia
And today on my birthday
I can proudly write
My name

MA COCCINELLE

You're like a ladybug, he'd say
Leaving me blushing
Yet not knowing why

Perhaps in thinking
I may have saved his soft-petal roses
Their downfall
Or even intrigued him
In some unspoken way

And after all these years
Of our union
Only now, do I ponder the comparison
For, my love, an entomologist
Adores the tiny creatures
        that many deem nuisances

So I guess I'm delighted
That my comparison is not to a flea

PATIENT AND DOCTOR

It seemed too far to remember
The laughter, the jokes
The late hours of explaining the illness
And wiping her brow
Amidst expressions of gratitude
For being there
Celebrating feast, battling famine

The papers shoved before him
Omitting those moments of caring
Conveniently

Too hard to remember the details
Leading to now
Uncertain if the fault is his to shoulder
With the weight thrust upon him

Yet the game has started
Without him
And the ball definitely rests in
      the opponent's court

Deciphering the motive proves challenging
For he cannot see her eyes
Concealed behind those deceptive shadows

The prospect of losing seems so real
Despite the truth, his truth as doctor

The court's volley has already begun
And what a nefarious match he foresees
With plaintiff and defendant
Both suited to win

WISHING WELL

I wish to
Restore you to the vibrant you
Put the sparkle back in your eyes
Place a smile on your dispirited face
Embrace you with hope and faith
Cherish the celebrated moments

Respect your need for calm and quiet
Listen to your myriad expressions
Understand your daily struggle
Light a candle to illuminate
      your path to wellness
Share your desire for healing
All the while
Seeking direction from the God who understands
Everything

COMFORT JUNK

Paperspaperstrinkets
Vestiges of times past
Not easily dismissed
Stored in plastic, paper boxes
For later perusal
That won't even materialize years later

Stuck in the past
For fear of discarding some invaluably valuable item
That has long been sequestered

And so with the antiquity
Comes stagnant comfort
(that boldly resists change)
And justification to hold on

Though the soul calls out for change
And the lips can taste the promise
The comfort of holding on
Is less risky
Than letting go
For some...

A FLY LIKE US

The tiny winged insect seems a bother here
Having avoided being swatted
Not once, but twice
While others treasure its very existence
Of thousands of genes
In deciphering the genome
Of the very human
That sought its demise

Yet the amazing thing remains:
How similar the nuclear substance
Between the two.
Despite their phenotypic dissimilarities
That Drosophila can lead humans
      to amazing discoveries
Is fascinating,
Is it not?

THUS SPRACH DIE MUSIK

I feel my music superior to yours
With rhymes chanting
Living beat boxes
And cellos carrying the bass
While airy staccato tunes jump out of the bassoon
Black and white keys mingle effortlessly
With melodic violas bowing
Pianissimo in sonatas
And brass, brass, brass
Saxophones tempt in sultry formation
Tunes improvised to the arias sung
In soprano
Lending tenor to the moment
In true operatic fashion
And horns blow with congas
Beating that mambo style
While the djembe speaks solo in
Call and response
With rhythms thought primitive to some
The smooth contralto serenades
About the child that's got his own
And electric basses slide
Hypnotically
To flashes of blue-green neon
Against the backdrop of the taiko
And uttered, though inaudible, words

Seductively, the sitar courts minor notes
And voices softly harmonize
A cappella, free form
I feel my music as yours
Speaking to choice
Simply music
Easily removing the superiority that divides

AGAIN AND AGAIN

Last night, I felt, between wake and sleep
A great joy indescribable
A moment of bliss
Exalt within me
As though heralding a welcomed renewal
And pondered the source
Or God within me
The feeling so magnificent
I dare say, a spiritual blossoming
Its abbreviated stay craved even now
And so, I'm left with the memory
Of then
Knowing that I would welcome it
Again and again

HER CHOICE

Some say the feeling is dull
And deep
Like indigestion, though different
Or sharp and piercing, intermittently
Like rewired electricity
Running unwanted up the neck and down the arm
Knocking the wind out
Breathless with the littlest exertion
Hungry for air
So, now while running
Her steps land hesitantly on the ground
In hopes of anticipating even arresting
        that heart-stopping moment

Stented once
She seeks activity
Though cautiously
And positively
Rejects the fear of movement

STANDING MISUNDERSTOOD

Where are the things that stood
Here
Despite the times
Plucked one by one
At her whim
Invisible to those who deemed
Her esprit ethereal
Her world intangible
Indeed immaterial

Where are the faces?
That challenged her faith
And derided her stance
On illusory concepts

Where are the words?
When spoken
Would pierce
And hurt her physical form
Avoiding her soul

Where are those who feared
That to understand her
They'd inevitably understand themselves
Without protective armor
Naked as when at birth
Without all their doubts

Revealed
As she had been...

SPARSE

Their hands
A hundred
Reached up
Above the bellies
Swollen with hunger
And want
Clothed in clean
Tattered garments
Barely uttering words
For the sound of their action
Lingered deafeningly
Amidst the flies
Swarming in the brutal
Scorching heat
Their faces gaunt
With eyes deep and piercing
And hair reddened

Sparse

As the necessities
That all should have

The twenty would lessen
Their hunger
Only temporarily
Though the image
Would stay
Permanently affixed

TIME WAITS

Tell me in
Heaven when
Every angel sings

Time
Halts
Outside my bedroom window
Unbeknownst to most
Gratefully
How precious the moment
That time allows
So selflessly, I eagerly

Follow the tune
Lifted gloriously
On
Wondrous wings
Even now, I laugh
Delightfully

Singly
Waiting
Impatiently
For
Time to again
Let
Yesterday

Play sweetly in my ears
Even
Now, I am tempted

To
Open my arms wide

Proudly embracing my guardian
Angel
Prepared to
Enjoy the
Rewarding experience that this brings

TO THE YOUNGEST MEMBER, NUMBER 27254-1

The rations looked every shade of gray
Odorless
Uniform as we had become
In symmetric metal and concrete rectangles

And every now and then
One would break the silence
Undo the monotony
Forgoing companionship
To sit singly
Accepting or refusing nutrients
Slid through channels
That allowed little light

All this for ruthlessly doling out injustices
Or adamantly resisting injustices
Payback for stealing another's life
A futile dare in exchange for gang acceptance
For pockets dusted with snow
The teardrop tattooed, a reminder
To the youngest member here

And all the while
The verdict hauntingly replays
Like a broken record
Two life sentences; parole denied
A choice unforeseen

Standing behind bars
We wait for life to offer us roses

ROOTLESS

I have come this far
From my roots
And find myself
Entrenched even deeper
Than in childhood

Detached
For long, I feel
The longing to be other than
I am
Standing, facing my reflection
And for the first time
I see
My roots
Searching for fertile ground
Around me

HE AND SHE (VI)

He whispered...
The words floated lightly
Evaporating the worry
Blanketing the sorrow

But the words would only stay
Temporarily

The departure inevitable

For it was she who usually knew the right words
And spoke them so easily
Embracing those in need

And now as recipient
Words alone proved inadequate
Lost in the vast void that remained

In this silent space, she knew that only
Time could diminish
The uneasiness that lingered in her consciousness

TO HER LIFE *–for Susan*

In this space
Words are heavy
Saturated few
The joy having been turned
Inside out

The tears serve as cleansing
Rain
Weeping words
Streaming down, down
Cheeks, moistening lips
Too leaden to speak

To the one whose parting is mourned
Now
To that one who would sing
And say
Celebrate life
Singing
Rejoicing
Breathing...

Here's to her life!

STEALING LIFE FOR LIFE

For ten months
She has been on this earth
Vulnerable to the fallacies of two
Who should protect her

Sacrificed ruthlessly
To regain what he feels
May be new life
As if her sanctity is his for the taking
As if her innocence could undo
The illness pervading his body
Even before her birth

Sadly his actions are sanctioned by some
Emblematic of the failure
To view all life as valuable

Her big beautiful brown eyes
Untrusting
The hurt leaking out of each pore
Of her expressionless face
Unsure if safety is certain
In the arms of the one
Who embraces her

DENTALLY SPEAKING

Let's talk about the ache that brought me here
Hidden behind my smile of pearly beiges and whites
Today
My mouth refuses to cooperate
And confirms this protest
By the drool that hangs down
Novocained, I feel good and embarrassed at the same time
Drooling here

The drill buzzes annoyingly. And what was a small cavity on film has metamorphosed into a crater, which my tongue can't help but slip into.

And honestly, for a few minutes, I wonder if there's been a mistake
Though I'm assured that the filling camouflages, no, fills the crater completely.
And "Look how perfect that looks"
(even though I cannot see deep in my mouth)...
Still numb

Sitting here,
The work now completed
My feelings mixed
I am reminded to resist those tempting sweets
that seem so ubiquitous and inviting

IT'S ALL RELATIVE TO WHOM?/REALIZATION I

*"Tiredness can't even begin to describe how
I feel right now..."*

Until I hear of her daily toil
With eight kids in tow
Her mini day camp
Most of whom attend school and after-school
    and weekend sports
That keeps her juggling
Time after time

Until I hear of his third job today
With breaks only rewarded while commuting
    from point a to b to c
All over again

Until I see her
Walking slowly
Anticipating the needs of the family
She loves
Leaving behind the family she gets paid to love
Only to awaken
Beating the subway rush
To greet her employer before eight

Until I chat with the elderly undomiciled gentleman
Searching for comfort
Laying across the metal grid
Smoking steam

Until I watch the thousands
Hungry
Walking miles away from the senseless warfare
And needless persecution

Until I truly stop and realize
The stark omission of rest and peace
       and comfort from the lives of many

CONNECTED

Imagine
Me and you
At a point
Lying connected
Life flowing from big to small
Miraculously

A hand places the clamp to cord
Forcing independence
And with ease I breathe
Thanking you

The remnant of this remains visible
On my body, the indentation above the pubis
Now a repository for lint
Or for a finger placed
Jokingly

Exposed purposefully
Pierced

This tuft of tissue reminds me
How connected we were then
And how connected we still remain
Without the cord
Between us

UNTITLED VIII/CONNECTED TWO

I am connected to God
Who is All
That is omniscient
Fearful, I need not be
Walking in the strength this allows
Gracefully

The reality of this is oh, so magnificent!

COMFORT

And some wonder why
I chose this—
His smile
Dimpled
Despite the white coat that announced
My presence
To listen to his heart beat

The red rubber and metal
Holding his attention
Only momentarily
When out reached his hands
Tiny
Welcoming
His mother standing there
Shocked

I reach, lifting him
As would his mother

He places his head
On my shoulder

Oblivious of the whiteness
That always frightens him

His mother smiles
Noting that he is smiling
Comfort—
Ably, still

COMFORT TWO

Amidst the carols
She twirls the thin curls
That frame the baldness
Of her father's head

The whimper starts softly
Eased as her mouth accepts the bottle
Willingly
He, maternally, cuddles her
In the seat of his arms
Rocking and humming
Naturally
And the comfort she feels
Is what he preaches about

Innocence is sometimes a blessing...

LEANING TREE

The leaning of the balsam irks me
As does the teetering of the glass
Placed there hurriedly
Somewhere, the forest weeps
Green
Baring the lonely void
Of one rooted up...

THE EXODUS OF HERE –*for Susan*

Everyone shouts,
Fight
For the children
And so I feel the struggle synonymous
With the pain and obligation
And desire and anger

And though my body feels heavy
And burdened
The want to fight occasionally dances
In my consciousness
Resonating between moments of lucidity
When what I speak, doesn't leave them puzzled

So hard it is at times
Facing the inevitable exodus
Of here
And remembering my initial desire
To win
Though entwined in expected denial then
So here I sit, propped up, knowing
They're here with me
And it hurts to have to leave
So soon

CHOICES

You choose and are chosen
To be
Many things to many
With aching tentacles
Far-reaching
Exposed
And desires strewn aside
To embrace the needs of those
Far more deserving
Than you

Stop now! Your thoughts
Are unwarranted
And will only engulf
The happiness
That you truly deserve
Continually stripping you bare
To reveal the tears
Locked in your heart
You need not be
Many things to many

Relax…

AWAITING ENTRY

I, like my closet, am cluttered
With unnecessary
Possessions
Forced commitments
Ill-fitting coverings
Old memories
Antique objects
Packed tightly and kept
The yearning to change
Sometimes effervescent
But coaxed down
Afraid of change
Though right here
I can hear the jubilation
And see the renewal
That taps gladly
At the door
Awaiting entry

...AND SO THE PROMISE WAS

And so, the time shall come
When you will stare
Not knowing me
Through the thin veneer
Our lips adjacent
Speaking to each other
The words undecipherable

It is in this moment
That I shall be prepared
To embrace you
Without questioning
Knowing that what was once
Is still felt deeply

Though presently
Our thoughts askance
Seek shelter here

And so the time shall come
When you will stare, not knowing me

It is then that I shall wonder,

What was your promise?

RENEWAL

The brightness of the day
Beckons me
Its breath crisp
With fingers dancing merrily
Caressing the tight curls
Seated gracefully atop my head

Dare I feign ignorance
Of the invigorating chill
Knowing that I've anticipated
The revitalization

Dare I shun
This electrifying bolt
That jolts my soul

How amazing in this very instance
That I feel renewed
Sensing the intention materialized
Shifting apathy into pure bliss

THE DREAM

I think the dream still flickers
Though the dust may have convinced
Some
Of its antiquity

I think the dream still whispers
Softly
Despite being hushed repeatedly
Vying for time
Against louder causes

I think the dream still stands
Its essence undeniable
Though physically dismantled
By doubt

Occasionally, it comes late
At night
To remind her of its presence
Indelible, unshakeable
Unwavering amidst the more transient
Fading worries that wish to cloud
Her vision

I know the dream
Still
Flickers
Whispers
Stands firm
Awaiting her desire to make it
Real

TOO LONG, IT'S BEEN

Too long it's been since we met
Overdue since your thoughts were spelled out
Scribbled words
One by one
Line by line

> Blank, I welcome the joy
> And sadness equally
> Massaging the ego

While you read the words
Placed here
Knowing them good
Tasting the veracity
Keeping the secrets jelled
In ink

> Yes, it's been too long
> Since you wove on me
> Words of beauty
> Frankness

Broad aquamarine stripes
Myriad shades of pink

How brilliantly golden
Your sun shines
Today

TÊTE-À-TÊTE

The place was plush
The wine,
Divine,
She continued on
And on, sewing the words
The needle boring the cotton

Batting his eyelashes rapidly as
Hers fluttered seductively
How light the moment felt
His words had been few
Too many uttered by her
The music of his warmth
The surreal tenderness of her touch
They wove
Quilting speechless now
Tête-à-tête

Two then
One
Then two…

SPEAKING OF LEOPARDS

That polka dot dress doesn't do you justice
Though you say it's your best frock,
Nonsense
That you feel feline
And powerful in it
Clinging to your hips
Provocatively

They whistle
Not because of the dots
Only to get you
Twisting in misconception

But in truth
Who am I
To judge your confidence?
Confident that my opinion should be
Accepted

That dress has outgrown you
And you it
Feline and all
The leopard thing no longer reigns

But this is only one person's opinion
Which undoubtedly is subject to debate

WE KNOW HER EVERYWHERE

Her beauty seemed long gone
She wore the hardship openly
Engraved on her brow

As if
This was expected
As part of motherhood
In her culture, she said

The words dribbled
Unconvincingly
And questions poured out
Effusively
A few stared, refusing to challenge
Or defend
The mores had stood the test of time
And today would be no different

She felt invisible now
Though once named beautiful
Clutching her sweater, she sat uneasily
Staring at its collar
And there, in tiny letters, read *Pretty Lady*
She smiled
The timing couldn't have been more perfect

FOOTTALK

My feet ache, something serious; right on the inside (the instep, I'm told). And all this week, I've avoided the pointed toe, narrow stilettos.

You know, the kind that looks twice the size of your foot: The kind that some find so elegant.

But then again, I've been pounding the platform. Shopping. Promenading. Just plain old street strolling. So you ask, what do I expect?

These feet constantly carry the weight and only naturally should force rest!

A NEAR COLLISION WITH NUNS

As fate would have it,
    the gray sedan reversed cautiously
Disguising the U-turn out of the
    convent's entrance

The oncoming van drove prudently
Per chance, by habit

Neither auto tooting the horn
A mere foot further
And the outcome would have been grievous

The four van occupants, all nuns,
    smiled unperturbed
While in the sedan,
    the driver's heart pounded, forcefully
How dichotomous, their reactions

The van slowly reversed
Allowing the sedan egress
Both drivers nodded in acknowledgement
    of divine intervention

WHAT THE BIRDS TELL THE BEES

The birds are spending an incredible amount
    of time chatting with the bees
Buzzing tones sauntering
Wings flapping effortlessly
Golden and black bodies framing vellum wings
Greet feathered flight

The flowers know
What all the buzzing is about

Something sweet lingers
Golden rich nectar
Perfect composition
Indeed not for the aerial ones
Who willingly announce through
    melodic diapason
While others flock to savor
This elixir of life

The birds and the bees exchange not words
Merely actions in their tête-à-tête
Keeping some guessing about the mystery
    of two in flight

WHITE ROSES

I smell the white roses'
Whispering aromas faintly
Leaning stems
Crossed deep down inside
The white water pitcher
On the bedside table
And she is missing their debut
Opening barely
Offering a glimpse

White rosebuds await their turns
Tight-lipped about their performance
Each one with purpose to soothe
And she is staring beyond them
As deep in thought as they
Standing stems in cool living water
Thriving
Knowing the right moment to bloom

HIATUS FOREGONE

The time has come
That pen should dance
Lead
To paper
With black strokes placed
Haphazardly
Erasing the ties, undoing
The knots
Defying conformity
And I should speak loudly
In words
Refusing to be silenced

REMINDERS

On some cold mornings
I've missed the touch
Of one
Lightly against my back
Whispering against my cheeks

Frosty-lipped
The chill tiptoes
Lightly against my back

On some cold mornings
I've missed the touch
Of one
Whistling against the window pane
Inviting a shiver

Reminders
That indeed, I'm alive

FOR WHOM

For whom do they sing?
In such loud voice
With silken robes
And velveteen shawls

For whom do they chant?
Simply garbed
All one, with shaven heads

For whom do they bow?
And stand repeatedly, reciting
In unison
Neither one glancing at the other

For whom do they weep?
Tears moistening their smiles
Hands greeting one another

For whom are they silent?
Staring as though in a trance
Perhaps transported in time
Transiently

For whom do they dance?
Feet rhythmically beating the ground
Hands flung skyward
Gratefully

For whom…

…The agnostic stares in wonderment
From afar

NED

His height challenged the very family
Whose name he bore
Being the tallest and the youngest
Thin and gangly
Like a straw, they'd say
And he hated the comparison
Finding it insulting
"He'd just hit a growth spurt, that's all"
"And his weight hadn't enough time
    to cling to his bones"
He'd heard his grandmother say this once
To a stranger
And wondered why she'd never shared
Her genius with the rest of the family

Now everyone questioned his love of sports
Of course, hinting
Basketball
Dissuading him from soccer
Too tall, even awkward
Some thought he'd be

Seeing the potential dollars

But he loved soccer and table tennis
    and scuba diving
Unlike his cousins who loved basketball
    and football
And craved his height

He'd heard his doctor use the word "Marfan"
Describing him to his mother
And he wondered who 'Marfan" was
Or even what it meant
Probable a synonym for gifted or athletic
Who knew?
He blushed
And wondered why his doctor
       hadn't complimented him directly...

DON'T SPEAK TWICE

Is it you who stole my calm?
Palm suffocating
Shaking me treeless
Leaving me lifeless
'Til the barren earth could weep no more

And bathed freely in my waters
'Til the sun transformed you
Into one of mine
And crawled belly to the ground
Fearful, your eyes darting side to side

And came at dusk
Clothed in peace
Your words as lullabies to my people's ears
You who were
One of us
Leader

The children followed
Inculcated and imprinted
Your Machiavellian temperament
As armor, protector of the cause
Munitions in hand
Brains washed deceptively

What demagoguery do you speak now?
Distant from us, forcibly
Having fooled us once
We who ignored your lust for power and greed
Were it not for one
Who strayed defiantly
What would have become of us?

What words could you possibly utter
That would allow you
To again conceal your intent
Disguise your character?

Smart sheep united
We refuse your lead!

AGING

It happens quickly, it seems
The gait tilted, forward and deliberate
The back hunched, just so
The smile still brilliant
Framed, wrinkles surrounding
And skin as delicate as vellum
Strands of silvery hair
Drape across her forehead
The once youthful bosom
Weightless, kneeling
Lightly kissing her belly
How time had changed everything
And thoughts seemed to quickly flee

She knew the progression
Necessary
Watching
Wisdom embrace youth
How some defied gravity's pull
Shedding twenty years, physically
Willingly reconstructed

But, in her
Stood sapience
Waiting to be tapped
She, having never tasted
The fountain of youth

GRAZING OUT OF THE FOLD

It must have been the words
That shocked me
The wattage so electrifying
To jar the heart-felt beats
Spoken so easily
In private
With regret repeated among the words
Though the eyes didn't match
Yes,
The eyes refuted the empathy

The constancy of this place
No longer mine to have
Unwelcome, I sat
Estranged from the fold
We who'd spent hours talking
Working
Laughing
No longer we
But me and them

So,
Moving on I must
Probably to greener pastures
But for now
I'll simply spend the time
Grazing
Out of the fold

SPELLBOUND

Incense nudges the innocent hairs
Bending resistance
Seductively
The sweet aroma wafts gaily
Down blackened paths
Its gust landing on buds
The taste bittersweet
The moment still
With eyes closed
Lost
Spellbound
And free to dream

REMINDERS II

On some cold mornings
I've missed the touch
Of one
Lightly against my back
Whispering against my cheeks

Frosty-lipped
The chill tiptoes
Lightly against my back

On some cold mornings

Whistling against the window pane
Inviting a shiver

Reminders
That indeed, I'm alive

WORK IN PROGRESS

This work has been in progress
For long
Balustrades and colonnades foregone
In favor of red earth and sand
The velvet drapery, an obvious contrast
       to the simplicity
Concealed
Behind

Red earth and sand infrequently seems
       unpleasing to the eye
Yet I keep it, as foundation
Sensing the uneasiness only
Ephemeral

You see, simplicity insists that its time be now
Grandiosity has had its day
And so the work continues
Surprisingly on schedule

Exchanging Pleasantries

CHALLENGED ON HILLSBOROUGH/ ARTFUL ENDURANCE

It struck me
So profoundly

Driving along Hillsborough
There—
Expressive amidst ceramic
Stood the presence
So deeply scarred
Solid oak robed,

Head bent
Pained with cross leaden
Embraced

The carving so real
To touch deep
Within and
Reflect torment and commitment and endurance
All at once

To be of one faith
And at its core
Transcend the finite,
Expose the common thread
Of suffering
Speak to beliefs varied

Artful endurance humanized
Yoked in religious verse

Of what do you speak, waxing sentimental, so?

In your spare moments
Just drive along Hillsborough
Open-minded,
Looking and seeing
Then,
Tell me what you think.

MADE-UP

His fingers paint
Shades of aquamarine just above the eyes
And supple pink
Outlines the lips
Soft black curls drizzle down
His forehead

Tall, shapely
Sequined in stilettos
Tapered and aching

In drag
Queen for a night

The mirror reflects him
As canvas

Self-portrait actualized

"Strike the pose"

As females stare...
Mr. Divine struts....

CEMENTED INERTIA

This mental block thing is
So familiar

Cemented inertia
Of thoughts coalesced
In stone

Infinitesimal quarks
As letters unseen
Frolic subconsciously

Ideas long craved
Doled out
Parsimoniously
The hunger
So raw
Each bite relished ravenously

At last
Freedom announces
Each molecule of thought
Mingles consciously
The bursts of energy
So welcomed

Unblocked mentally,
My composition just flows unperturbed...

NOT ALWAYS EASY TO IGNORE

You step slowly into the elevator
My hand pushing "Door Open" courteously.
I see the fright, etched in your face,
Of me, calm and relaxed.

Chance has augmented your fear
As we exit together,
Hesitant, you question my purpose here

"No, I do not work here."
Your steps seem even more uncertain, now
Unbelievable that I should live here—
Your neighbor

Indignant at your remarks
I soon realize how prejudice
Dictates your life
How insular and stagnant your views

I ignore you, for now.
Lucky you,
I'm in no mood to debate today.

COOL DRAFT

Pen short
poems
that can be
read with feeling,
felt with purpose,
devoured with glee,
and guzzled like a tall cool iced tea
on a hot summer's day.

COUCHED THERAPY

You say
I'm angry
Having never lived in my
World

Each session when we meet,
I lie sprawled on your couch
Buttery-soft mahogany leather
Embracing

My dreams recited
In hypnotic beats
To your monotonous nods

I feel my wings
Unclipped, empowered

Weightless
Soaring high,
I say
The time is now

Yes,
Now is the time
To simply be

PRESSING ONWARDS

He with
Repressed wants
Suppressed words
Oppressed soul

And me
Impressed by his ability
To press forward
Despite the odds

He stands mountainous
Undeterred by meager means

Aware of the impact
His presence reveals

Stepping purposefully
Two naked feet
Leaving imprints
Outlining the path

Faith emerges from deep within
Peering out through his pores
His tenored voice
Electrifies

He with
Body
Soul
Words

To me,
He seems depressed
No more;
Just stately to behold

GOLDEN LOTUSES

At 8
The knife carves deeply
As drums sound out the piercing
Cry
And life-force and pleasure
Diminish in some ritual ploy
Her sanctity destroyed
Foretelling years of pain and anguish
Dictated by culture's erotic reinvention
Anatomical birthright
Mutilated
In whose idea of beauty?

At 4
The cloths woven and
Wrapped tightly
Repeatedly
Disfigure the foundation
On which she stands
Golden lotuses in three to five inches, perfumed
Placed in petite, flowered
Silk covers
Tiny feet
Sanctioned to ensure marriage
Stand as erotic reinvention
Ritualistically disguised

Two women
Maturing in pain
Spirits strong
80 years old teetering in tiny footsteps
50 years old feeling hollow
Retelling their stories
Recounting their lives

...And who dares to speak
Labeling their hurt
A necessary tradition
Having never experienced this hurt?

THE MIRACLE OF YOU

Have we shown our delight
At having you back?
It seemed for a moment
That you had left us,
Even you said so yourself

Oh, how we missed
Hearing your voice
Wise and learned
Sharing your life
Seeing your smile
Enjoying your laugh,
Your humor so contagious

The miracle of you
Still leaves us astonished

Everyday,
We sing,
"Welcome back home to wide-opened arms
Welcome back home to wide-opened arms"

MOON PEACE

The moon has put on her sunscreen
Disguising whether she's one-quarter
   or one-half here
Donning rose-colored spectacles
Watching airborne dancers leap across the sky

For now, she ignores stares
Lost in the interlude
That enchants her

Forecaster that she is
Though in her moment of respite
Now refuses to answer our curiosity

In time, midnight calls
Producing its blue-black essence
And clouds fold
Whispering their 'good nights'

Soon, she'll unveil her true self
Glistening bright with the stars

ADOLESCENCE CALLS

Wasn't it just yesterday
She reached out to you
Holding hands to cross the street
Her tiny hand one-fourth yours

Just yesterday, it seems
She ran to you
Tears streaming down her face
Waiting to be
Kissed and hugged
Soothed by your assuring touch

And
Now here she stands
At fifteen
Challenging your every word
Tapping her well of rebellion
Expressed in attitude, clothing and speak

Adolescence offers her the gift of independence
Your one-on-one talks
Not always her priority
As you vie for time to remind her,
"Stay grounded!"

In her,
You see you reflected, plainly
Similar childhoods, one generation apart

Wasn't it just yesterday,
You hugged her fears away
Kissed her tears dry
Tucked her in at night
Reminded her of your love

Just yesterday...
It seems...

SINCE SEVEN

Draw your rapier
To fight the demons that linger
Inside you
Forcing your mouth to speak
Nonsensical thoughts
Conversations recited that urge you
To defy law, order, life

At your lowest
The temptation to acquiesce
To voices echoing in the hollowness
Between your ears
Forces tears to dampen your face

Since seven
They offered a safe haven
As you fought to maintain
Your innocence from falling
Prey to unwanted invasion

Draw your rapier
Dueling steadfast
Soon raising your arms contentedly
Claiming yourself
Victor
Of a match well fought, indeed

UNTITLED V

...And why write
Themes of sadness, fear, hurt
When love, peace, faith
Can heal
And salve the deepest wound
Caress the shattered heart
Embrace the most troubled
Cure the wounded soul?

Do you believe for one moment
That in showing sadness, fear, hurt
And pain
Our eyes are compelled to see
Our minds forced to witness?

Compelled to see
Forced to witness
That peace and joy
Are but mere manifestations of love,
        unconditionally?

Do you believe that love conquers all?
That love in its naked form
        engenders harmony, still?

ADJUSTING THE FOCUS

Look at how your camera peers
Into my space
Digital flickering
Evident of modern techno-dreams
That you harbor
Warped among the convolutions of your brain

Listen:
The *Do Not Disturb* sign
Pertains to you and others who avoid
       asking for permission

How dare you
Download my privacy
For your viewing pleasure

Caught red-handed?
Lost for words, are you?

EXCHANGING PLEASANTRIES

"My plans are all ????ed up"...she said
"What the ????...he said
Casual conversation spoken easily
Heard just out of earshot
—I walked towards the metal detectors—
"Your boarding pass, ma'am,
and one piece of I.D.
Please consolidate your bags.
Thank you."

How interesting to me, the dichotomy of speak
Yet commonplace to these two
Security personnel now politely directing passengers
Rushing to catch flights
Oblivious
And me reminded of the eff's word
Utilitarian role in our vernacular
Inserted as a master key
Unlocking thoughts and feelings
With purposeful inflection and emphasis

I walked towards the gate,
Questioning their action—
Impertinent
And my reaction—
Incredulous
Looking through their lenses
I thought:
Just a simple, powerful word
A harmless pleasantry exchanged
between three

FOLIAGE UNVEILED

Photo
Synthesis lies dormant
As nature displays her palate
Of pleasant auburn, yellow, red richness
Painted with broad strokes
Ushering autumn into view

Fall foliage, forcing stares
Lightening moods
Uplifting spirits

Change couched in color
Signaling nutrient storage
As leaves prepare for fall

Winter soon will come
Offering cold clear icicles
While some branches will remain bare
Their leaves falling
Succumbing to the earth
Fertilizing and ensuring growth

Nature announces change
Seasonal change in cyclic formation

Change—
So necessary for life

THOUGHTS ON RELIGION

The church is split
On the appointment of a bishop—
Because some say, heterosexuality
        should be a benchmark
For one's rise in ecclesiastical leadership

Ironically, the beliefs of some religious types
Who cannot see past sexuality,
May be blatantly antithetical to the
        very teachings of the One they worship

For,
Are we not challenged to love others as ourselves?
All connected we are
On Earth
Though sometimes blinded by thoughts
        of superiority,
We preach

Sometimes finding forgiveness hard to accept
And sometimes hard to give

…We are often judging,
while refusing to ourselves be judged.

CREATE

Why curb your creativity?
Letting pragmatism take
Center stage,
Abandoning your dreams
To fear

Take charge!
Explore the artistic talent
That lies within

Discover you
Creating uniqueness
Resisting stagnation
Accepting change
Forgetting limits

Let your imagination dazzle you,
My dear!

WHAT WAS, IS

Climbing up this treehouse
I can sit for hours
Letting my feet dangle high above the earth

Reaching just above
To hold a cloud of moisture in my palm
Satiating the thirst inside

Setting my imagination free
To sway and twirl ecstatically
Feeling the cool winds caress my face
Enjoying the placidity that
Night brings
I smile deep inside

Climbing down
I find myself
Feeling more grounded
Energized by the experience
That just was

...That just is...

OXYGEN ROCKS

I open my mouth wide
To take in the breath
That nourishes my soul

My tongue rolled out
Like the red carpet
Reserved for dignitaries
Each tooth standing guard
Fortress and welcoming party

I smell the breath of oxygen
And feel it coolly
Touch my face
Invited to walk this red carpet
That clings to its every particle

The welcome so perfect
I feel it everywhere
And anywhere
This nourishment that penetrates
My core
Just rocks!

GOSSIP COLLAGE

Oooh Girl,
I hear my ears buzzing
Your lips tapping a rhythm
Juicy, salacious and generous
All at once
Thrown haphazardly
Against canvas—
A collage of gossip, praises and critique
All in the same breath

Now you know
Those ears welcome the talk
Soaking it up like
White bread would some sweet wine

Giiirrll, your audience can't wait
To hear the latest news
As if their contentment
Depends on it

Gossip so sweet
Even irresistible
Like an addiction
Slowly tearing them apart at the seams

Girl,
What d'you just say?
Slowly tearing whom apart at the seams?
What?
Don't you go getting deep on me, now...

LIKE LOVE

From like, To like vibrates learns evolves unfolds turns true love

FRUSTRATION

It's not so simple:
We work side by side
Talk openly
Laugh loudly
And you assume
I'm always accorded the same rights
As you.
I demand equality, as I should
While some call me
Angry
For insisting on
Respect
And open-mindedness.
These discussions aren't spoken
Often
because
It frustrates—
The fact that some apply
Restrictions to my colored skin

Out of fear
Of the diversity
That is
The human race

IT AIN'T ILLEGAL

At this very moment—
I feel like I'm tripping
Off of life
Got the adrenaline thing rushing
Through my veins
Rejoicing and praying
I'm blessed

You see this here high
Ain't illegal
It's just natural endorphins
From spiritual awareness
Of who I am,
Satisfaction at
Where I am,
And willingness
To keep learning
And accepting
What I could become

WORLDLY THOUGHTS

The world could use:
    A soothing massage
    A meaningful hug
    Chamomile tea in a gigantic mug
    Love in all colors of the rainbow
    A fragrant relaxing bath
    Morale boosting
    A child's imagination
    Fewer egos, more love
    Being tucked in at night
    Friendship
    Eradication of greed and hate
    Peace
    Being held and rocked to sleep
    Excitement that doesn't destroy
    Nurturing
    A passionate kiss
    Best friends
    A balm that numbs pain
    Caring parents
    A joyful fiesta and restful siesta
    A sage's wisdom
    Reciprocity and support.

The world needs us to be:
    Realistic
    Loving
    Compassionate
    Joyful
    Peaceful
    And
    Thankful beings.

PERCEPTIONS

The talent she has
Of looking and seeing
You
Is startling, when you first meet

And there is no fanfare
Nor regalia
Announcing the talent

The gift accepted
Without self-aggrandizement
Without trumpet call

So you wonder
If she can read your thoughts right now
Or predict the next minute
And stay focused in her own self

Admittedly, you are impressed
By her ability to transcend the now
And maintain her uniqueness and style

Guided by spirituality, she seems
Graceful

THE SMALL DIVIDE

The idea that memory could be lost
Even fade slowly
Is a scary proposition:
That forgetfulness could overwhelm—
Leaving one to dwell in the past
Lose touch with reality,
With the here and now
With their place on Earth—
Is a frightening thing

For we know ourselves
Even define our purpose
Often by what we sense, feel, see, hear
And where we are, now.

To watch
An adult revered
Wandering and expressionless
Living with only brief moments in the present
Is so hard to grasp
So incomprehensible to accept.

The fact that we feel like outsiders
Unrecognizable to the very person
    who may have nurtured us
Is one difficult pill to swallow.
That memory lost
Can discombobulate us
Just speaks to our frailty as humans
And underscores the thin line that divides
Living in confusion from living sanely,
    as we know it.

KISS GOODNIGHT

That 19- inch Sony
Is babysitting Baby Brother tonight
A chore, I've been assigned for the past week

He sits, maybe, one foot away
And stares so intently at those cartoon characters
Doing the impossible

Right now, I can't play with him
'Cause Justin should be calling any minute
Plus Baby Brother should be asleep anyway
He had his snack—
Ranch-flavored Doritos and
    that red-colored water he likes
Says it makes him strong like Junior,
Our 22-year-old brother, who likes mixing
Red Kool-Aid with tequila—
Says it makes him strong for the girls

Junior's always complaining that
I should read or sing to Baby Brother,
    or something
Hell, he's the oldest:
I don't see him running to read to Baby Brother

Yo, all I know is
Thank God for the Sony
Baby Brother should be 'sleep now
With those sticky fingers
All over Mama's couch

Yup, just as I thought
I'm gonna kiss him goodnight
Right on the forehead
—He says it tells him I love him
He saw it on t.v., once

DUST TO DUST

He craved the whiteness
Of dust
He believed able to dismiss fear
Conjure up an imagination
Wild with excitement
Elevate him to a shaky pedestal
Where high
He claimed himself invincible

Fine lines
Taunting
Spilled
Forcing him to grovel
In search of tiny particles
Lost on cold alabaster

Lines driven to the heart
Reworking the electrical control there
The vibrations generalized
Shaking him into disbelief
The white fist clenched tightly
Usurping breath
Revealing him slave to white dust

NEUTRAL DELIGHT

Perhaps, the most gratifying part of
    these field trips
Is watching his dimpled cheeks
And seeing his 5- year- old body
Speak joyfully
As the car moves forward in neutral

For him, exhilaration starts
From the moment soap squirts
Rolling with water on the windshield

His laughter reaches high
As strips of sponge and revolving brushes
Greet our 2000 Volvo

For a moment, he is entranced
Moving in sync
To the rhythm played out
On the windshield

As sponges hug and slide
Leaving the Volvo squeaky clean
His delight crescendos
Revealing a smile so priceless

He needn't thank me in words
His joy is plenty enough
And for this alone, it's worth every penny

THE CALL GIRL AS PARASOMNIAC

The funny thing is
I don't even know his name
Although we have met and spoken for hours
And dreamed separately of the future together
Even rehearsed nature's secret pleasures

It seems strange
That someone should know you
And not really know you
That one person may live two lives
Talking and holding you in one moment
Then rushing off hurriedly in the next

This blindfolded exchange
That we share
No longer feels secure
No longer will suffice

It is as if we are sleepwalking
Living with both eyes shut
Never questioning the reality

Today
I must ask him
Who he really is

COLÈRE

That one thought—
Actualized
Prompts its initiation

Warmth rising
Surreptitiously metamorphosed
Into a steamy, vibrant rage
Spiraling and shaking me inside out
Deceiving my heart to pound
Fiercely

I feel its stronghold
In tornado-like fashion
My thinking being the last bastion
To surrender
And soon, my lips are uttering words
In four letters
Louder and louder

Loudly, I fall prey to this emotion
Despite previous promises of resistance

The provocation was intended
To incite the demise of my calmness

The perpetrator claims victory
Having released negativity
And usurped an ounce of my
Positivity
Even if only temporarily.

RETREAT

The gentle touch of your fingertips
To my skin
In moments wanting
Of your caress
With lips lightly brushing
My nape
Enrapts me in this warm comfortable love

For hours, we rest just so
With no words uttered
Yet ridding our minds
Of entangled stress

In this place
This retreat
Of surrender

That omits worry and pain
I hear my name echoed tenderly
In harmony with
Yours…

TAINTED

Pangs of aching rip through my stomach
Like a drum maestro banging drums
Pain twisting and hiccuping
The drum majorette marches on
This aching so disharmonious
Not consonant with my brain
Leaves me helpless, depleted

Here I sit barely
On the bowl
With jets and streams of liquid ejected
From below
And with each propulsion
The hiccuping inside gets louder
The band just marches on

Outside, is as drab and cold
As I feel
Though, I know this too shall pass

To think
One bite of nourishment
Tainted
Sent this body into intestinal convulsions
Usurping practically every ounce of strength
In continuous waves

Thoughts somersault
In my search for control
Fading fast in this tumultuous struggle

Then
Quiet
The band is slowing its march
The majorette only twirls lightly
Gradually coming to a halt

Rest beckons
As I fall, fatigued, to bed.

BIRDS LIKE US

By the brook, we would sit
As kids
Casting sandstone pebbles
Creating ripples in the liquid stillness

This is where
We spoke of dreams
And fantastical futures
Laughing and rolling
In the grassy plains
That shielded us from
The earth's hardened sod

And sang off-tune
Skipping and dancing uninhibited
In the cool midday air

And once, we questioned
Why the robin sought to retreat here, too
Nested high in the abundant
Verdant foliage

But perhaps, she too sought to
Create ripples in the liquid stillness
Just below.

HONEY TO ME

Your love
To me
Is like honey
Straight from the comb—
Golden
Rich
Sticky
Pure
Unadulterated sweetness.

THE BATH CALL: I

Burgundy, shag plush encircles the feet
As though a prelude...

The luxury of each step
Excites his senses
And soon, the terry cloth tumbles
As each toe feels the liquid warmth

Slowly, his body conforms
To the lavender fragranced water
Hidden under heaps of bubbles
Covering every inch
Of his fatigued physique

The mood is so right
So private
With dimmed lights
And he alone, as planned

Liquid calmness
Transporting him to serene enclaves
Massaging away deep-seated stress
Leaving the body light
Liberating the mind
To dream uninterrupted

These baths
So rejuvenate and center him,
Nourishing every degree of his soul

He loves when she prepares them for him
How luxurious they make him feel.

THE BATH CALL: II
Burgundy, shag plush encircles the feet
As though a prelude...

The luxury of each step
Excites her senses
And soon, the terry cloth tumbles
As each toe feels the liquid warmth

Slowly, her body conforms
To the lavender fragranced water
Hidden under heaps of bubbles
Covering every inch
Of her tiredness

The mood is so right
So private
With dimmed lights
Scented candlelight
And she alone, as planned

Liquid calmness
Transporting her to serene enclaves
Massaging away deep-seated stress

Leaving the body light
Liberating the mind
To dream uninterrupted

These baths
So rejuvenate and center her,
Nourishing every degree of her soul

She loves when he prepares them for her:
How luxurious they make her feel.

WELCOME, LIFE I

You knock
And I question
Whether to allow or bar you
Entry into this temple
My eye glued to the peephole
Hoping to magnify and see you
In full 360-degree form
Fear keeps my hand from turning the knob
And courage struts by encouragingly
Fear dictates that when admitted, you
Wield power and control, leaving a soul
Captive and enslaved
Reason argues that, like clay, you
Should be molded and crafted into beauty
So the soul can look upon the handiwork
Saying proudly,
This is art of me
Guided by truth
Directed by God.

WELCOME, LIFE II

You knock
And I question
Whether to allow or bar you
Entry into this temple
My eye glued to the peephole
Hoping to magnify and see you

In full 360-degree form
Fear keeps my hand from turning the knob
And courage struts by encouragingly
Fear dictates that when admitted, you
Wield power and control, leaving a soul
Captive and enslaved
Reason argues that, like clay, you
Should be molded and crafted into beauty
So the soul can look upon the handiwork
Saying proudly,
This is art of me.

SEEING THE GOLD COAST

The red earth homes stand unadorned
Perched on this rugged plateau
Practical at this moment
Yet, vulnerable to Mother Nature's whim

The sky, dressed in hints of pink and teal
Hovers just above the green lushness
And we can see the land for miles

A spring, just down the path
Unexploited, flows calmly, it seems

We are here to build homes
And stand in awe of the natural beauty
That is this place

And in our travels of this rich land
Embraced by the culture
Our time here celebrated
By dances and ceremonies steeped in tradition
We are aware of the simple elegance
And royalty that live here

Too soon, we share in history's enslavement
Freedom shackled in deep dark dungeons
      of shame and pain

Unimaginable!
The story told brings tears and heaviness to many—
Unable to grasp the cruelty inflicted by humans
Some say, the spirits have lingered here
Visible to certain eyes

The memory of this
Stays for many

We are here to build homes
How ironic that we feel just as vulnerable as the
    red earth homes we will leave behind

The land here is rich and dusty
And paved and bustling
The contrast that is the city
Western in architecture and dress
Leaves many feeling at ease

The country, the city
Sights to be explored
Yet, what impresses most is the heritage
    and beauty of this land

That emanates from the pores of its people

We are here to build homes
And will leave changed in many ways.

*Gold Coast–Ghana

REFUGEE CAMP
–dedicated to the Liberian refugees at the Buduburam Refugee Camp, Ghana

Displaced people
In the midst of deprivation
Raise their voices high in jubilation
"Amazing Grace, how sweet the sound"

Like banyan trees
Sprouting branches of hope
Rooted deeply in the belief that
Goodness will prevail

Escaping civil unrest
Leaving tangibles behind
To settle here
Living piece by peace
Peacefully deprived

They have been named "refugees"
Distinguished from those born here
Similar in appearance
Struggling to be the melting pot

Their dwellings lie clustered
With areas of relief sometimes
Announced by the stench that drifts
Unwanted in the air

My people
Have lingered here and endured

With an unshakable faith that eases the suffering
With ambitious plans
    and fantastical dreams that unify

With hopes of a future homecoming
With thoughts of never returning
Living day to day
Piece by piece
Escaping civil unrest
Leaving tangibles behind

My people have lingered here and endured much
Through faith

THE MULE

The impregnated condoms went down easily
One by one
Jostling with the acidity that laid waiting

He realized the wealth that had lodged
Deep inside his belly
Like a human vault
Worth millions to some cartel

While, to others, he was simply a mule
Used
Strictly for transport
He detested the word used by the Americans

His quest for more urged this risky adventure
The desire to dip in this golden pot
      of opportunity
Welled up inside him
Only once had he entertained
      the thought of ruptured condoms
Don't dwell on it and it won't happen—
      his elders had always said

Traveling undocumented
Narrowly escaping arrest,
      buried in one of eleven barrels
This was reserved for the truly courageous—
      the bosses often said
Think of the mouths you can feed;
      your financial wellbeing; your future

And here, as if by magic, his future
    dangled right before his face
As he stared deep into its eyes
Never once had he thought his offspring
    would find the drug so desirous,
    so addictive
Craving it ounce by ounce

How ironic it was:
That he had escaped death from the very substance
That would claim the lives of his two sons.

OASIS

My thoughts lie
Shipwrecked on this oasis
Having sailed on neutral and choppy waters

Navigation has never been my forte
My compass barely a guide
My sixth sense leading me here

My journey began with thoughts
Entangled
First, rowing against the tide
With life vest securely fastened

With time, rough, wild waves acquiesced
To gentle ripples...

...And now,
My thoughts seem cultivated
By this fertile earth

Shipwrecked on this oasis, I am
Dancing with the sun
Watered by the ebullient spring
That welcomes renewal

PRESENTLY PRESENT

Everyone can live the pleasure of feeling
Their spirit—
The true naked form that is you
For what determines this honor
Is whether you are here
Awake in your reality
Presently present
Or hidden in the past
Afraid to encounter the real
You
Stop for a moment
Only to listen to yourself
Only to be yourself
Present in the now

SOULFUL PLAYING

Your fingers just glide smoothly
Across the whiteness
Gently caressing the blackness in between:
As if you are lost in the intimacy—
Echoed as sweet melodies that announce
Your creativity

Music enchants and
Invites

And you, the creator
Can reach even those who stick cotton wicks
Deep in their ears
Pretending not to hear the sound

Your music transcends the tangible:
Colorblind, colorful rhythms
Seep deep into the soul
Planting a gentle kiss
On the soul's open lips

UNTITLED VI

The product of the two was beautiful
Innocent
And a constant reminder of the menace
That slept in her body

She spoke in hushed tones
Intentionally keeping the father in the dark
Questioning and accusing him of sharing
unwanted blood with her

The infant smiled—
Free from the menace
At least for now
Beautiful bright brown eyes
So phenotypically similar to his proud papa

So ironic, for had he not been born
His mother, too, would have been
        intentionally kept in the dark

So innocent, this infant
Yet a reminder of the secret
        that the parents kept from each other
Positive, they were, that neither one knew the truth

THE EYE'S MIND

Oh, Eye!
You celestial body
Sitting orb
Delicately couched in orbit
Looking out
Reflecting colors, form
And all that is present

It is you, who speaks to me
And compels me to witness
It is I who can peer
Deep into the soul
Through your myriad expressions

In commune with the mind
It is you who can see what is
And what isn't
Complex creation, you are
Even to those who are blinded
With touch, the possibility of seeing
    with eyes closed
Remains endless

27 YEARS

Look at me
And see twenty-seven years of our life
Shared
Equally and unequally
Lived
Blissfully and selfishly
The commitment sometimes difficult to keep

The beauty of our love
So powerful
The occasional hurt so flabbergasting
The joys so exhilarating

Wisdom has taught us
To love for the moment
To appreciate each other
Pain has taught us
To embrace change

Cognizant of life's cyclical nature
And the challenges that togetherness brings
Today we stand
Unwavering
As one

INADVERTENT MIXING

Being so careful with this procedure
And just a simple slip of hand,
The thin millimeter metal bores right through
Ignoring my screams for universal precautions

Pain and anger rush through me
From the point of contact
Expressed in one single word—
SHIT!

The warm reality of tiny volumes
Of unwanted blood, mixed
Of unknown transference
Jolts my calmness
Sending possibilities spiraling
In my mind

This 6-month-old infant
By history is nascent
Free of threatening virions

So in regaining my composure
I am relieved
As my body instantly defends itself
From unwanted invaders.

A PEARL IN WAITING

What fine work you've done
Today
Despite the lack of praise
Without adulation showered upon you

See the beauty of your handiwork
Unfold yourself from the impenetrable
 shell of modesty
You so proudly display

See the pearl that you are
Luminescent treasure
Precious indeed

Ignore those who fail
To recognize your worth,
Who highlight your insecurities
Belittling your choices

Can you not see the gift that you are?
Your talents a mere reflection
Waiting to be nurtured

Soar high
For the world patiently awaits your promise.

A KISS IS NOT A KISS

Funny that some would quicker kiss a stranger
In a bar
Than give breath to a stranger
Fighting for life

Though both require the touching of lips...

One is usually done pleasurably
While the other implies the role of Samaritan—
Responsible for a life besides one's own

Admittedly, kissing is unlike resuscitation
That one act can seem so frivolous, so desirous
Even passionate
While the other implies duty, community
        and compassion
Highlights their differences, it seems

Yet both originate from desire—
Desire to enable life
And desire to enable like

BEAUTY IN WOOD

She chose the antique piece
For its value, age and beauty
Its decorative mirror vividly reflected so much
The ochre handles unique to the piece
Exhausted from years of use

Each inlay of worn pecan, cherry and zebra wood
Needing inspection
Needed to complete
The whole

She imagined the beauty of the piece
    once restored
Leaving admirers
Speechless

She chose the piece
For its value, age and beauty
And now reflected within it
Was the restoration that would mean
    endless possibilities
For her

ON SEEING THE DOCTOR

Listen,
I'm only two
And already I've been stuck, probed
       and poked countless times
Once, my thigh got pinched four times
And then some water got squirted inside
I overheard the doctor's excuse—
To protect me from creepy crawlers

Yesterday, my body began to shake for no reason
And it felt like my skin was on fire
So we ended up there again
Four people stuck me eight times
But I refused to share my blood with them
Since they caused me pain
And ignored my tears
I did drink that orange liquid
And that made me all better

My twin sister is a ham, my mother says
But I thought we eat those on holidays
When we visit the doctor
The ham smiles, lifts up her shirt
Even opens her mouth wide,
       when they stick that yucky wood inside
And never squirms when that
       black plastic triangle is pushed in her ear
What are they looking for anyway?
Seems like they're fishing

No one really asks permission to poke and probe
Only once, a doctor asked my permission
And actually explained,
        even though her tone was condescending
I haven't seen her since
She must have been fired for going against the code

Anyway, the bottom line is:
Going to the doctor is no trip to the zoo!
Yes, I'm only two and already protesting
NO HAM, I AM!

WHAT AN ORANGE REVEALS

The 9- year- old orphan, forced head
 of household,
Who has survived destruction and
By fate gained wisdom past his years
Is thought unconnected
To the heiress, designated head of household
Whose fortune seems guaranteed for generations

The butterfly, fanning its wings
In the lush Costa Rican rainforest
Seems unrelated
To the Australian koala riding its mother's back

The juniper berries growing
In Hungary
Seem isolated from the maize
Cultivated by Inca descendants

The terrain decimated by bombs
Across the globe
Seems so different from the town
Swallowed by monsoons

But appearances can be deceiving
Even in oblivion, we are all inhabitants
Of this spherical planet

And what rattles a part of the sphere
Undoubtedly rattles the whole

DOCTOR AND PATIENT

Hesitancy lingered in the air
Between them
Billowing like thick gray smoke
Visible to both

Her lips stuttered
Syllables stumbling over one another
Spewing a reality hard to conceptualize

The discourse replayed
In her consciousness
Like a scratched 45, abandoned

The second test had proven inconclusive
And required a third for confirmation
And then another...

Placing her hand on her breast
She hoped to enter unannounced
And steal this surreptitious, uninvited guest
To which she played host
Unknowingly, until now

She lay waiting for the perfect moment
And willpower
To completely rid her body of
      the encapsulated fear
As only she could do

THINKING IN VAIN

Vanity is so much a part of humanness:
A salute to our ego-driven thoughts
      of me, me, me.
That human form should be marred
      and mocked is often unacceptable to us,
especially, if we are to suffer the pain.

To have a part of the physical form removed
      unwillingly and often in protest,
is an experience that most wish to avoid.

That the taking is done to another, is a reality
sometimes difficult to entertain,
even if the taking is purportedly done to save life.

40 AND...
You're 40, right?
No, can't be!
You look so young.
Married, right?
Why not? You're not looking?
Wait... You're engaged?
Miss, you have any kids?
So the biological clock is ticking—
Tick-tock-tick-tock
(Whoever invented that clock
 must be rolling in dough)
So, like what do you do? No husband, no kids?
You must have lots of money—
A career girl, working hard? No?
Where's your house, condo?
You've got to buy...come on...time's flying
What are you waiting for?
You're 40, right?
Want a date, baby?

You have got to be kidding, right?

CHANCES ARE...

You're lucky to be spared mishaps—you think—
As a backseat passenger
In this yellow metal mobile
Quickly accelerating 50 mph
In midtown
Bouncing in and out of craters
Nearly slamming into the car ahead
The working seatbelt quelling the anxiety

You look at the rearview mirror
And see the image of a lotus blossom
Strategically placed to calm nerves
Rattled by this New York cabbie
Determined to reach your destination
Yesterday

You flagged this cabbie down in midtown—
He seemed pleasant enough
So you assumed a contract of safety,
Never wanting the thrill
Yet, for you, this has been a high-speed,
    expensive adventure
For him, a mundane drive

Chances are, you consider yourself lucky
Having escaped any mishaps
On this unexpected escapade

FEAR MOVES SLOWLY

These uneasy thoughts
Inch in
In the quietest of times
Even to the brave and bold lion
Whose place commands silent respect
In the hierarchy

The turtle-paced emotion
Saunters confidently
As if challenging the bravado
Of the fearless giants that lie waiting

The disguises have proven successful
Cloaked in anger, apprehension
Inhibition, jealousy
Even love

But in this kingdom
We see it for what it is—
Fear, skillfully disguised

DOCTOR AND PATIENT 2

He speaks in 'isms' and 'ologies'
As if speaking commonly would lessen
    the meaning of the words
And he, the patient
A testament to 85 years of living
Sits bewildered
Watching lips move briskly
Hearing nothing
Nodding in agreement
Because tradition teaches that these 'healers'
    are all-knowing learned professionals
...And some are audacious,
believing their way the only way

These monthly visits have
    remained unchanged for twenty years
The doctor's soliloquy undecipherable
    to the patient's ears

Traditions are hard to change
when neither participant sees the need
    to truly communicate with the other

CHAMPAGNE SLINGBACKS

Right now, all I can think of is comfort
Oh, I know I look good
In these elegant champagne slingbacks
The compliments have been non-stop
With everyone staring
Admiring how they hug my feet
Accentuating the contours

The truth is
I've made three trips to the restroom
Seeking respite
And there, massaged my aching corns
As my feet screamed out in relief

I've avoided dancing
And socialized only briefly

As my girlfriends say,
"This is when vanity supercedes comfort
and pain takes on a new meaning"
Even in pain,
I have to laugh at myself—
Just styling and aching

LOVE-JOY

And what of this love
That you have welcomed so graciously
That leaves your mind topsy-turvy
Weaving boldly
Displayed as that twinkle in your eyes
And enlightened glow on your cheeks?

What of the joy
That radiates in your eyes
And emanates from your pores
There for all to see?

Your blissful smile tells all

This love speaks in syllables
Infectious
Poetically knitted with receptive lips
Recited openly

How exciting that this love can be
More than just romance alone

PATIENT & DOCTOR

She stopped in at least bimonthly
Her laundry list of ailments
Painstakingly scripted on lined paper
Waiting to be addressed in their
    twenty-minute tête-à-tête

His stethoscope hung loosely around his neck
Greeted her coldly
The reality of this softened by his
    compassionate touch

To him, her visits here were solely
    to ease her loneliness
Agoraphobia had nearly consumed her life
Just two years ago
Paradoxically, despite her age
Life was beginning again
And their rendezvous was the catalyst
    to effect that change

DOCTOR AND PATIENT 3

At 37, his life reflected
20 years of working, providing, sacrificing
and playing
Breathing in tar, digging ditches
Drilling into cement
Drilling into rock
Drilling
Drilling—
The reverberations felt in every cell of his being
Jarring his neurons

Naïve, he had eagerly accepted the task of drilling
The machinery violently shaking his body
The vibrations quelled with ethanol

At 37,
Standing and walking depended
        on the titubations and tremors
That heralded his movements

At 17, he dreamed freely
Two decades later, his one dream was for a cure

Today, he hoped this doctor had answers
Could even dispense a pill to quiet
        the agitation inside
Or offer words both positive and hopeful

Optimistic about his chances
He sat patiently shaking
Waiting to be seen

WHOSE REALM?

Can you imagine Alzheimer's
as blissful
to him?
That his wandering may be in a realm
 incomprehensible to us
yet pleasurable to him?
That initially he struggled to be here
Constantly
For *there* engendered angry feelings in us
Inadvertently transmitted to him
There allowed sadness and tears to well up
In our eyes
Visible to him
For we wish to feel connected to
 and not forgotten by him
We wish him *here*.

...If only we could whisper
deep into his mind
and question whether happiness abides *there* still...
Would it be easier?

RED RIVER RUNNING

At 12, the dampness arrived unannounced
Ushering in another pubertal milestone

This life-water had been contained until now
Only running in closed channels
And now, it flowed plainly
Its expulsion soon to be routine

It seemed that womanhood had called
Yet her actions still remained
Steeped in childhood
The change in body just blossomed
Practically overnight

The river she felt was a reality
      that women spoke about
Often attributing their emotional swings
      to its presence
This was the secret her friends had whispered about
Behind closed doors

Anticipating its arrival
She greeted this change, calmly

TREASURED TRUTH

He thanks me from the bottom of his heart
As though there lies the seat of treasured truth
A testament to the appreciation
    painted in his dimpled smile
And I, in turn, graciously welcome his thanks

As is often customary
With usual words
Insisting his gratitude unnecessary

And it is only now
In these quiet moments
When cynicism forces a second glance
    at the expression—
Summoned in opportune moments to express
heartfelt gratitude—
That I question
This bottom of his heart

Reserved, is it?
Or conveniently used as a thoughtless reference?

Quite frankly, I usually prefer the top
But this bottom of his heart
May indeed hold treasures
May indeed be promising, still

THE INVITATION

The invitation specifically read 'cordial"
Dinner at seven

What had it been?
Ten years since their last encounter
Unfavorable, as it was

Unbelievable that after seventeen years together
They willingly signed
Parting amicably
Their differences so blatant, that they wondered
    what attracted them in the first place

The invitation, itself, seemed unpretentious
Handwritten with the Waterman nib
She'd bought him for their first anniversary
Sentimental, she thought—
But only for a moment

Putting cynicism aside,
She would dress as if this were a blind date
Expecting no fireworks, no fanfare, no hoopla

She flirted with the possibilities
    of leaving him dazzled
...Hmm, she could just taste it...

THE QUESTION

Grief crawls within, necessarily
Revealing words unshared with the parted
And hurt knotted tersely
Occasionally unravels through tears
Unwillingly shared

Guilt too lurks within, unnecessarily
And feelings of betrayal leak out tearfully
In times of solitude

And so the questions flow
Did the embattled warrior stand courageous?
Alone
Even in the midst of perceived defeat?
Did acquiescence, even abnegation
    of responsibility
Enable the parting so swiftly?

Could the struggle ultimately have been won
When its reality was never shared?

LIFE AS DANCE

DANCER ENTERS STAGE CENTER
And finds it difficult to swallow this life
    in large moves
Preferring to taste in deliberate steps
Occasionally preferring hunger
    when the choice seems too real to bear

DANCER PAUSES, FEELING UNEASY
As the curtain is mistakenly lowered
Leaving her and the audience with voices raised
And angered emotions

If courageous, the dancer could
    raise the curtains high

And commence with moves
    even more beautiful than before

Life occasionally deals a hand
Difficult to embrace
But the belief and desire to persevere
Far supercedes the urge to accept defeat

Life need not be swallowed as is
But should be danced fearlessly

BONE CRY

They don't live this illness
Of bones pained
Crying out
Of vessels crowded with humpbacked passengers
Sickled, gasping for air
With whites of eyes stained yellow
Staring back in the mirror

And yet,
They name me addicted
To natural and manmade endorphins
When my want is only for understanding
And relief of this bone-piercing pain
Expressed in moans
And taut lines furrowed deep in my brow

Can't they see that my dreams are just as theirs
When this illness allows me respite?

Can't they see that my hopes exist
Just as theirs?

HEARING HER

With mouths agape
And words of 'how'
The hearing of her cancer
Rests uneasily on the tongues

And in this time of offering words and thoughts
Of optimism
To buffer the reality
Of feeling distorted
Life seems palpable

And in grabbing to hold on tightly
The supports are galvanized
Despite the realness of falling

For the test
Unexpectedly is difficult and now
And even though the words may prove elusive
Among the tears

Listening is, sometimes, all that may be asked for

MORNING ROUTINE

So routine
This washing with water
In rushed hours of early morn
Announced by monotonous beeps
And melodic sounds

With eyes barely opened
And bodies dragged
Often unwillingly from rest
Each trickle of pure clear wetness
Awakens sleepy pores

And, as time quickly passes,
The realization of work is so urgent
To some
That the enjoyment of water
To skin is missed
…So routinely

ENGAGED

Engaged
She is
With ring to left fourth
Finger
Refusing party affiliation
Engrossed in stimulating discussion
With her partner, who too
Announces their intention with
Words concealed in metal around
The left fourth finger

Both engaged mutually
In words and symbol
Politically charged
Without apprehension or concern
For those preaching against
Who deserves whom

Engaged
She says
With feelings entrenched
Deep and personal
Refusing party announcements
With metal and words
Woven
And ample

NOTHING QUITE LIKE IT

In one moment
She was strutting
Confidently, without a care in the world
Each step taken for granted
Its placement on the ground assured

And in the next,
Each step proved unmanageable
As its placement sent
Shock waves up the spine

The backbone stood still
Processing the unremitting pain
That demanded stillness

There was nothing quite like it
This back pain
That curtailed locomotion
That called for hot and cold
And rest
And time

Nothing quite like it
This stubborn ache
Abruptly leaving the backbone
Lying still

WISHING YOU HERE

This day
Here
Minimizing
the distance

each part of me wants you
in words

of oceans, lands and sky

Wishing
What separates us

my hand could hold
deep in its palm,
And touch the realness
Of you,

This day
Would acquiesce
Simply
Willingly

As if the mind
would paint you
in memories

Drawing the contours of the you
I once embraced

This day
Here

each part of me feels you
in words

QUESTIONING YOU, QUESTIONING ME?

Silence isn't golden here
In this space
Of doubt and blame

Eyes locked in do-si-do
The quiet preempting the strike
Like some hyena stalking its prey

The anticipation of both
Is that of conflict
Unveiled in questions posed
And questions forged
With neither answering the claims

The moment stands still
The hyena leaps assuredly
In midair
The prey narrowly escapes

The moment thickly lingers
Checked-mate.

FIFTH GRADE BLUES

The fifth grade teacher, Ms. Shaw, wonders why
I fall
Asleep in class
Despite the crowd and noise
Though quieter than home
And still excel

My grandmother's adage has served me well
"Stay in school, even if you fall asleep doing it."
"You're my brightest light bulb, Paul."
We lived together, 'till she walked to heaven
And now living with my twenty-six-year-old
        cousin is tough.
You see, he's nocturnal,
        loves celebrating just about anything
And sleeps most days
Just like his friends

So my best rest comes in school
Right after lunch
Which is why I stay after school
Packing in the knowledge and doing homework

My cousin deceptively tells Ms. Shaw
        that I stay up at night
Flipping channels
I think she knows he's lying
And I'd like to blow his cover
To flip him one
But I keep quiet

And slowly count the years
Until I'm eighteen

WISHING YOU HERE (#2)

This day
Here
Minimizing
the distance
As if
What separates us

Would acquiesce
Simply
Willingly

Each part of me
could feel
You, here

each part of me wants you
in words

of oceans, lands and sky
my hand could hold
deep in its palm
and touch the realness
of you,
If only the mind
would paint you
in memories
drawing the contours
of the you
I once embraced

each part of me could speak
gratefully in words

HEAT RISING

350 degrees of heat rising
Tempering the 40 degrees in the three-room,
    cold-water flat
Winter is sometimes the toughest
The most intimate
With bodies huddled for heat
Like blankets in some landlord's linen closet

Even with five kids
The gas range stays propped open
Leaking fumes and warmth

The Gas Company has been here twice
When carbon monoxide leaked, they say,
Into our blood
Sadly, we thought
The headaches were from hunger

But despite the danger of propped
Oven doors
And this extended frost
Instinctually, we know to stay just far enough
Away
Risking getting burned for comfort

The landlord promises heat
Shivering with hands out for rent
Then climbing into her heated Lexus

The boiler's been broken now
For months
The price of gas has doubled
So heat comes to us
Four hours a night
And we huddle seven tight
On the mattress
On her kitchen floor

CLASS REUNION

Why didn't you come?
Vanity stood, silent, behind pursed lips
Then mechanically spewed out
Her usual soliloquy of illogical
Ifs, ands and buts

She had to be stopped—
I whipped out the Polaroid snapshot
And in one second, her laugh
Rang out, uproariously

We had all matured
Perhaps even gotten wiser—

Lathan, still with that comb over and
        funny as all get out
Saul, pretentious, spoke ad nauseam
        about his financial coups
Kwaku, traded textiles, traveling extensively
        across the globe
Simply Divine, we always found her name
intriguing
        and she believed she was
And Ten, namesake of the number of offspring
        her mother bore:
I mean, her mama could have been more creative
Lim, still had that eclectic style that spoke
bohemian
        and defied her heritage
Ram, no longer lanky and nerdy, owned some
upscale,
        uptown eatery with his partner
Remember, Therese?
Married with three kids and quite the expert
        on collegiate games
Oh... And Leah owns a performing arts school—
No surprise; that girl could move that body
        and belt out a tune

Our little Tuesday Club ain't too shabby, huh?
Class of '81
The memories were good, weren't they?

So, really, why didn't you come?

LATE NIGHT DRIVING

Seated inside you
Our movements become one
Rolling
Down dark winding roads

You know,
These late night drives deliciously leave me
Wanting more

Exhilarating enough

To make our hairs stand on end
As we meander
Through highs and lows
Basking in the cool night air's refreshing touch

The moon peeks its head forward
Nodding at our playful romp

Seated in you
Driving even 30 miles per hour
My heart laughs
Loudly
One beat at a time

SON TO FATHER

My father has this pride thing going on
Working for little or nothing
Now for twenty years
Loyalty and work ethic, he preaches
"Son, I can do this job with my eyes closed"
Yeah,
And barely have food to eat

A brilliant stupid man, I call him,
Behind his back
He tells me, not my mother,
His check is garnished
Child support for two other children
That he can keep well hidden
If payments continue

We sacrifice for these two
And my mother wonders:
His working long hours for so little pay

I see it eroding his ethic
Tearing him apart
His countenance and posture
Bent

Pop, I remind him, first, loyalty to self
Then to others
"You're a kid, what do you know,"
his diatribe usually begins
Not today
He's honestly too tired
Yet willing to listen
Pop, I say
But already he's nodding

DEFIANCE

Though barred from entry
This stubborn pounding
Sits purposefully atop my head
Conqueror
With tendrils osmotically insinuating
Creating a vice-like grip
Around my skull

Slowly creeping down my neck
Consonant with each heartbeat
The rhythm drummed out
Defying protest

Refusing defeat
We spar for hours

My epée foiling the plans to linger
Endlessly
Rejected, the pounding abates

Defiant, with epée advanced
My head feels clear once more

LITERARY GROOVE

These words flow like
Luther's smooth tenor
Cascading rhythmically
Floating elegantly
Like Grover's, "Mister Magic"
Tunes snaking in and out
Massaging that warm spot
Meant for moments like this
Provocative like Nancy's silky, romantic
"With My Lover Beside Me"
Ooh, oui!
Play it again
Just sing it again
Let my words flow
Rhapsodically
Like your grooves

WELL?

Has the well run dry
Despite want?
Tongue parched
Like desert sand
Longing for
Tiny drops of transparent wetness
Falling deep down
Inside the cemented stomach

Water resisting evaporation
Stumbles
Landing purposefully
Welcomed by hungry lips

And soon
The torrents will reign
Thunderously
And that is when the grand celebration
Will begin

Dancing in praise for water

Author's Notes

A friend recently asked me about my next book, specifically whether it would be poetry or another genre. Well, here it is. *Being in Two Volumes*, a combination of two poetry books, *Balancing Act* and *Exchanging Pleasantries*. All of the poems were written during 2003–2005. I'd thought about including excerpts explaining some of the poems, but later thought it best to leave the poems open to the reader's interpretation. Delve in, explore, laugh, cry, reflect, critique as you wish. I hope you enjoy the poems as much as I enjoyed writing them.

Note: The Chinese character on the front cover is "FU"—blessings, good fortune.

I would like to thank God, my family and myriad friends who continue to love, support and encourage me.

Thanks to Walter Gray Lamb, the graphic designer, who captures my poetry beautifully through design. You are talented!

Thanks to Liz Haak, my gifted editor.

Thanks to Abner Kohn and Jay Street Publishers, who published my first book, *Poetic Moves While Doctoring*.

And thanks to you, the reader, for supporting my work.

TO PEACE and LOVE.
ONE PEOPLE.

www.ingramcontent.com/pod-product-compliance
Lightning Source LLC
Chambersburg PA
CBHW032114090426
42743CB00007B/348